BASEBALL BLOOPERS

WORLD'S FUNNIEST ERRORS

Bill Gutman

Troll

Contents

Introduction

Baseball has always been America's game, the *National Pastime.* Of all the major sports, it is baseball that has the longest and most glorious history. There were legendary players cavorting on the diamond more than one hundred years ago, and there are still legendary players today. Despite major changes over the years in every facet of the game and its structure, baseball endures. For many people, it is *the* rite of spring, when players report to training camps in Florida, Arizona, and California to prepare for another season.

It seems to be a simple game: You throw the ball; you hit the ball; you catch the ball. Whichever team throws, hits, and catches better usually wins. Baseball, however, involves a lot more than that. It's a thinking man's game that requires savvy in addition to great athletic skill. As one manager tries to outfox the other at key points in a game, the players must execute a complicated routine of strategies and moves.

And then there is the unexpected. Maybe more than any other sport, baseball invites a variety of bloopers. An errant throw, a pebble on the field, a base-running blunder, a big pitch thrown to the wrong spot, an opportunity missed, a dropped ball, a promotional gimmick gone awry, a crazy bounce of the ball taking it where it wasn't supposed to go—all these factors contribute to the overall character of the game. They have produced moments that are amusing and funny, puzzling and often virtually unbelievable, sometimes sad and, in a few cases, even heartbreaking.

To a large extent these crazy stories from the diamond enrich the history and tradition that make baseball a uniquely American sport. The exploits of so many great players down through the years— Cobb, Ruth, Gehrig, DiMaggio, Williams, Mays, Aaron, Koufax, Rose, Bonds, Maddux, Griffey—are known to all genuine baseball fans. But not even the all-time greats can avoid an occasional blooper.

Even less well-known players have earned a place in baseball history, thanks to their rather peculiar nicknames. Read a book such as *The Baseball Encyclopedia* and you meet players called Snooker, Fido, Bald Billy, Goobers, Slewfoot, Fidgety Phil, Tookie, Bootnose, Suds, Foghorn, Skabotch, Sloppy, Squash, Noodles, and Satchelfoot. Think some of these guys were involved in bloopers or unusual stunts? You bet.

Baseball has such a long history that it would be impossible for any one book to capture all the strange things that have happened on the diamond. But *Baseball Bloopers* proves, once and for all, that the game involves much more than throwing, hitting, and catching. Not a single element of the sport escapes becoming an adventure from time to time. For every home run, there is an error. For every stolen base, there is a bonehead play on the field. For every run scored, there's another that should have been scored. In other words, on the other side of every great play is a blooper.

Chapter 1

Some Wild and Crazy Plays

Let's start with some of the nuttiest plays that have ever occurred, where suddenly the norm gives way to near chaos. Sometimes a single player's blooper can turn a normal play into something never before seen. There's no predicting when such plays might happen, though some of the rules and customs from the earlier days of the game made them more likely to take place. Here are some examples of baseball's wildest and craziest plays.

Maybe the Shortest Home Run Ever

A pop fly is usually an easy ball to catch. If it's high enough, a fielder should have plenty of time to camp under it for the grab—unless the sun is in his eyes or another fielder thinks that *he* should catch it. Pop-ups that fall in no-man's-land often result from miscommunication between the fielders. But perhaps no pop fly did more damage than one hit by the Washington Senators' Tom McCraw on May 17, 1971.

The Senators were hosting the Cleveland Indians at Robert F. Kennedy Stadium in Washington, D.C., the year before the franchise moved and became the Texas Rangers. In the fourth inning, the lefty-swinging McCraw hit what looked like a routine pop fly over shortstop Jack Heidemann's head and into shallow left-center field.

"My ball, my ball," yelled the backpedaling Heidemann. At the same time, center fielder Vada Pinson came charging, trying to holler Heidemann off.

"No, I've got it," Pinson shouted. As if that wasn't enough, Cleveland left fielder John Lowenstein decided that he had the best shot at catching the lazy fly and began yelling the other two off. The formula for disaster was complete.

Any one of the three men probably could have caught the ball, but none had a chance. Just before it came down, all three fielders crashed together and crumpled to the ground. McCraw's pop dropped to the grass, rolling just a few feet away from the fallen trio. Seeing the collision, McCraw kicked his trip around the bases into high gear. Second baseman Eddie Leon raced out and picked up the ball, firing it to home plate. But McCraw slid in under the tag for an inside-the-park home run!

The injured Indians players had to leave the game, both Lowenstein and Heidemann on stretchers. Heidemann had a concussion; Lowenstein, a leg injury. Pinson staggered off but needed nine stitches to close a cut on his face. What began as a routine play on a simple pop-up resulted in a massacre of Cleveland players—and one of the shortest home runs on record for Tom McCraw.

As John Lowenstein later remarked, "That was no ball McCraw hit. That was a bomb."

Passed Ball—Run!

One of the great cases of mistaken identity occurred in a game between the Houston Astros and the Atlanta Braves in the late 1960s. Norm Miller, a Houston outfielder, was on third base with the Braves' reliever Cecil Upshaw on the mound. Upshaw didn't want the run to score and was working carefully. He fired a low, outside fastball for which Atlanta catcher Bob Didier had to lunge.

Suddenly, a white object went spinning away from home plate, toward the backstop. Houston's third-base coach, Salty Parker, figured it was a passed ball and shouted to Miller to run. Thinking the same thing, Miller wasted no time breaking for home. As he thundered down the line, he wondered why catcher Didier hadn't run after the ball. He found out when he went into his slide and a disbelieving Didier simply stepped up and put the tag on him.

The bewildered Miller looked more closely at the "passed ball." What he and Salty Parker had thought was the baseball was a small white plastic cast that Didier was wearing to protect an injured finger.

Upshaw's fastball had knocked the cast right off Didier's hand, but the baseball remained squarely in his mitt.

"Boy, was Miller ever embarrassed," said one of the Braves. "He was a sitting duck, and there was nothing he could do about it."

The Kid with the Glove

One of the great things about baseball is that you never can predict how a game will turn out. You don't know who will be the hero. Perhaps the most unlikely hero ever to emerge during a big game was a twelve-year-old boy. Well, maybe he wasn't exactly a hero in the classic sense, but for New York Yankees fans, he was the toast of the town.

It was game one of the 1996 American League Championship Series between the Yanks and the Baltimore Orioles. The bitter rivals were meeting at historic Yankee Stadium on October 9. As usual, the two teams were in a close battle, the Birds leading the Bombers 4–3 in the bottom of the eighth. The Yanks' rookie shortstop, Derek Jeter, was facing the Orioles' Armando Benitez with one out when he hit a long, high drive to right field. Tony Tarasco, playing in right, went back to the wall and reached up as if to catch the ball.

At the last second, a glove came out of the stands right above Tarasco's outstretched arm. The glove belonged to twelve-year-old Jeff Maier, a Yankees fan from New Jersey. The ball hit the boy's glove and was guided into the stands. Umpire Rich Garcia signaled home run, and the argument started. Right fielder Tarasco claimed he had a bead on the ball and was just waiting for it to come down.

"Me and the kid almost touched gloves," he said. "It was a routine fly ball, and there is no way in the world I would have dropped it."

Umpire Garcia said he did not think the fan interfered with the catch. But after looking at the replay, Garcia admitted not only that the ball would not have gone into the stands if the youngster hadn't touched it, but also that he probably should have called fan interference—although he said he would not have called the batter out. The bottom line, however, was that Jeter's fan-aided homer tied the game, and the Yanks' Bernie Williams won it with a no-doubt-about-it homer in the eleventh inning. From there, the Yanks went on to take the series.

Would the outcome have been different if Tarasco had caught Jeter's high drive? No one will ever know. But it is certain that the Yanks had a tenth player helping them that night: a twelve-year-old boy with a quick smile and a quicker glove. All of New York hailed him as a conquering hero.

A No-Hit Nightmare

The dream of every big-league pitcher is to have, if only for one day, super stuff—all his pitches working, pinpoint control—and to throw a no-hit game. Even if a pitcher doesn't accomplish a great deal in his career, if he throws a no-hitter he'll always have that moment to savor.

Journeyman Ken Johnson achieved that goal one day in 1964. But for him, the dream turned into a nightmare—because of one play. Johnson, who would end his career with more losses than wins, was pitching for the Houston Astros against the Cincinnati Reds on April 23. Although he would wind up the year with an 11–16 mark, Johnson had it all going that day. A dream game. He was retiring the Reds inning after inning without giving up a single hit. The problem was, going into the ninth, Houston didn't have any runs, either. The Astros were being shut out by Joe Nuxhall.

In the Cincy ninth, Pete Rose tried to break up the no-hitter by bunting. Johnson raced off the mound and picked the ball up in plenty of time to get the speedy Rose. But while his control to home plate had been outstanding, his throw to first wasn't. It sailed over the first baseman's head for an error, allowing Rose to reach second base and then to gain third on a ground out. When second baseman Nellie Fox committed another Houston error, Rose raced across home plate with the only run of the game.

Nuxhall completed a five-hit shutout, while Ken Johnson made history of his own. He became the only major-league pitcher to throw a no-hit game . . . and lose!

Ball Four Starts the Merry-Go-Round

Here's a crazy play that involved one of the great ballplayers of all time. It happened on June 30, 1959, when the Chicago Cubs were playing host to the St. Louis Cardinals at Wrigley Field. Cardinals superstar Stan "The Man" Musial was at bat, with Bob Anderson pitching for the Cubbies. With a 3–1 count on Musial, Anderson fired again. The pitch was low and away, and it skipped past catcher Sammy Taylor, rolling to the backstop.

Stan "The Man" Musial was one of the great hitters in baseball history. But a simple walk against the Cubs in 1959 resulted in a blooper that brought two different balls in play, with Musial tagged out by the "right" one.

13

Umpire Vic Delmore called ball four, and Musial began jogging toward first. Instead of retrieving the ball, catcher Taylor and pitcher Anderson began arguing with Delmore. They claimed the pitch had nicked Musial's bat for a foul tip. Ball four, Delmore repeated, and the argument continued. Upon reaching first, Musial saw the players arguing and realized time hadn't been called. With the ball still by the backstop, he broke for second. Cubs third baseman Al Dark quickly raced to the backstop to pick up the ball.

At the same time, umpire Delmore pulled a new ball out of his pocket and, without thinking, handed it to catcher Taylor. Seeing Musial headed for second, Anderson grabbed the ball from Taylor and fired it toward second. Simultaneously, Dark picked up the original ball and threw it to shortstop Ernie Banks, who was a few feet to the left of second. Anderson's throw flew over the bag into center field. Seeing the ball go into center and not knowing there were two balls in play, Musial gleefully broke toward third. Only he ran smack into Banks, who tagged him with the original ball.

Now confusion reigned. Players from both teams began arguing, and the umpires had to huddle by themselves. Finally, Delmore acknowledged his blooper in putting a second ball in play. But since Musial was tagged with the original ball, he was called out!

If you can follow the flow of this crazy play, you really know your baseball.

The Tape Measure Single

When it opened as baseball's first indoor, domed stadium, the Houston Astrodome was sometimes called the Eighth Wonder of the World. During a game in 1974, Phillies slugger Mike Schmidt must have wondered why they built it at all. Schmidt was in his second season and just beginning to make his mark as one of the league's top young sluggers.

One evening in June, the Phils traveled to Houston to meet the Astros in the Dome. In his first at bat, Schmidt got a fastball, took a mighty swing, and caught the ball just right. He knew immediately the ball was going into the center field bleachers and slowly started his home-run trot. No need to run hard.

Out in center field, the Astros' Cesar Cedeno, one of the best in the business, didn't even move a muscle. He, too, knew by the sound that this ball was going into the seats. So did all the fans. In fact, everyone knew . . . except the Astrodome itself. The ball was an estimated 300 feet (91 meters) from home plate and about 117 feet (36 meters) above the turf when it suddenly stopped in mid-flight and fell straight down to the playing field.

Schmidt, taking a slow trip around the bases, had just passed first when the ball landed. He stopped in his tracks, mouth open in bewilderment. He had no choice but to retreat to first as one of the Astros picked the ball up and fired it to second. Then everyone realized the impossible had happened.

The stadium's designers had assumed that no

Though Mike Schmidt hit 548 home runs in a Hall of Fame career, none may have been hit harder than one in the Houston Astrodome in 1974. Unfortunately, that titanic blast hit a speaker hanging from the dome roof, fell back onto the field, and left Schmidt with a long, long single.

hitter would be powerful enough to send a ball up to the dome, but Schmidt's blast hit a public address speaker that was suspended from the roof. Under stadium ground rules, the ball was still in play. According to some observers, the ball would have gone more than 500 feet (152 meters) had it continued into the seats, but Mike Schmidt had to settle for a single. In fact, it was probably the hardest-hit single in baseball history.

"I think people will start to realize that I'm around now," Schmidt would say afterward. Though he retired with 548 home runs, Mike Schmidt would always remember the homer he didn't hit—or was it the homer he almost hit? Maybe the homer he should have hit? Let's just say it was the homer that was foiled by the Houston Astrodome.

A New Meaning for "Bases Loaded"

This is one for the books. The former Brooklyn (now Los Angeles) Dodgers were playing the former Boston (now Atlanta) Braves back on August 15, 1926, when one of the wackiest plays in baseball happened—one that all but killed what looked like a big Dodger rally.

It was the seventh inning, and the Dodgers had loaded the bases with just one out. Up to the plate stepped rookie Babe Herman, who was already a .300 hitter and four years later would hit .393 for the Dodgers. Sure enough, Herman picked out a fat pitch from George Mogridge and slammed a drive toward the right-field fence. The three base runners waited to see if the ball would be caught, but Herman just put his head down and ran full speed.

The ball bounced off the right-field wall. Then Hank DeBerry, the runner at third, scored. But pitcher Dazzy Vance, who had been on second, slowed down as he rounded third and seemed confused. Chuck Fewster, running from first, had just about caught up to Vance. But he, too, had to slow down or he would pass Vance on the base paths and be called out.

Suddenly, Babe Herman came thundering toward the other two runners and looked as if he would blow past both of them. Third-base coach Mickey O'Neil started shouting at Herman, "Back, back, back!" But Vance thought he was shouting at him and suddenly raced back and slid into third, where Fewster was already standing. At almost the same time, Herman—head still down—slid into third from the second-base side.

When the throw came in to Braves third sacker Eddie Taylor, he looked at the strange scene and licked his chops: Three Dodgers were standing on third. Taylor just smiled and tagged all three. The umpire had no choice. Vance was the only one entitled to the base. He called both Fewster and Herman out, ending the inning.

Herman was officially credited with a triple, but in one of baseball's wackiest plays, he had tripled into a double play—and the Dodgers wrote a new definition for bases loaded. For years after, if someone said the Dodgers had the bases loaded, the standard answer was, "Yeah, which one?"

Hey, Babe, This Isn't the Time to Steal!

Even today many people claim that Babe Ruth was the greatest baseball player ever. The Bambino's

714 career homers account for only part of his fame. Before becoming the game's premier slugger, the Babe was a highly effective left-handed pitcher. He was also a solid outfielder and clever base runner in his prime. In other words, he excelled at all facets of the game.

The great Babe himself, however, once pulled a bonehead play that was so dumb even a raw rookie wouldn't do it. Its effect was compounded because it happened during the seventh—and final—game of the 1926 World Series, when the Babe and his New York Yankees teammates were performing at their peak.

The St. Louis Cardinals had battled the Yanks tooth and nail. In the top of the ninth, the Redbirds held a 3–2 lead, and the Yanks had three outs left. Aging mound star Grover Cleveland Alexander was pitching, trying to coax one more inning out of his tired old arm. He got the first two Yanks out, and then the Babe stepped up. Alex knew Ruth could tie the game with one mighty swing, so he pitched the big guy carefully, finally walking him. As Babe trotted to first, Alexander still had his work cut out for him. Coming up was cleanup hitter Bob Meusel, with young Lou Gehrig waiting on deck. Both were powerhouses who could also end it with one swing. Only they never got a chance.

As Alexander made his first pitch to Meusel, Ruth suddenly took off for second. No one had given him the steal sign, and the Babe wasn't all that quick. He had had only eleven steals all year, yet incredibly here he was—in the last inning of the last game of the World Series—his team trailing by one run and with two outs, trying to steal second.

Cards catcher Bob O'Farrell almost froze with surprise. He couldn't believe the Babe was running. Then O'Farrell fired a shot down to second baseman Rogers Hornsby, who was waiting with the ball as Ruth slid in to second. The Babe was a dead duck. His poor judgment gave the championship to the Cards, and that was the only time a World Series has ever ended on a stolen-base attempt.

"[Babe] didn't say a word," Hornsby would later recall. "He didn't even look at me. He just picked himself up off the ground and walked away."

Yankees owner Ed Barrow always remembered Babe's blooper. "It was Ruth's only dumb play of his life," Barrow would often say.

First Find It, Then Field It

Who says the ball doesn't take funny bounces? Just ask Dutch Leonard, who was pitching for the Washington Senators against the Philadelphia Athletics on August 1, 1945. Leonard was in the midst of a two-hit shutout in the eighth inning when the A's Irwin Hall lined one of the Dutchman's knuckleballs right back at the mound.

The ball hit the pitcher in the stomach, and he covered it with his glove as he doubled over. When he straightened up to throw the ball to first . . . he couldn't find it! The ball had disappeared. Leonard began looking around frantically, trying to spot the ball on the ground. Still, no luck.

Suddenly Leonard felt something in his pants leg. Apparently, the ball had slipped inside his shirt when he bent over and slid down into his pants. Irwin Hall was laughing so hard he didn't get any farther than first base.

History repeated itself just three years later when the A's were playing the Boston Red Sox. This time the Sox's Billy Goodman slammed a hard grounder to short. The A's Eddie Joost reached down to field it, but the ball scooted up his sleeve and fell into his shirt, settling at his waist. Goodman was safe at first. But Ted Williams, who was on third when the ball was hit, was laughing so hard at the sight of Joost scrambling inside his shirt for the ball that he forgot to run home.

Playing Baseball or Shooting Pool?

One of baseball's funniest plays occurred way back in 1914, when a group of men tried to start a third "major league." It was called the Federal League and lasted just two seasons. Like many new leagues, it experienced a shortage of cash and had to operate on a shoestring budget.

During a game in 1914, only one umpire showed up. By calling balls and strikes from behind the pitcher's mound, he could also make the calls on the bases. Because umps didn't carry extra baseballs in their pockets back then, a supply of fresh baseballs was placed in a tight group alongside the ump and behind the pitcher.

The problems began when a hitter named Grover Land lined a pitch right back up the middle. Wouldn't you know it, the ball hit the stack of extra balls and scattered them like a break shot on a pool table. The balls flew in every direction, with the one Land had hit lost amongst them. Each fielder grabbed the ball nearest to him and tried to tag Land as he romped around the bases.

Who knows how many times Land was tagged by the time he crossed home plate? The problem was, no one could prove which ball was the one Land had hit. Umpire Bill Brennan had no choice but to rule the hit a home run. Soon after, some bright baseball official decided that it wasn't a good idea to leave a bunch of extra balls on the playing field.

Bending the Rules

In 1957 the Milwaukee Braves were playing the Cincinnati Reds when Reds third baseman Don Hoak shocked everyone by fielding a batted ball while he was running the bases. No, Hoak didn't forget which side he was on. He decided to bend the rules to avert a possible double play.

Cincy had a potential rally going. Hoak was on second, and another Reds player was on first with none out. Big Wally Post came to the plate and promptly hit a crisp grounder toward shortstop Johnny

22

Logan. It looked like a perfect double-play ball, a rally killer. That's when Hoak got into the act. Running toward third, he suddenly stopped in front of Logan, bent down, and fielded the grounder barehanded.

For a few seconds everyone was confused. They thought Hoak had freaked out, since the rules stated that a player hit by a batted ball is automatically out. By fielding the ball, Hoak was out—but now there was no way the Braves could complete a double play. Instead of a runner on third with two out, Cincy now had runners on first and second with one out.

Hoak's clever little play led to a rule change. The next year the rule read that if a runner fielded a ball to avert a double play, both he and the batter would automatically be called out.

Hey, I Thought I Hit a Home Run!

Though no one could have known it at the time, a bonehead play early in the 1931 season cost the Yankees' Lou Gehrig the home-run crown that year. It happened during a game on April 26 against the Washington Senators. New York's Lyn Lary was on first base with Gehrig batting. There were two outs. Sure enough, the powerful Gehrig slammed one of his vicious line drives toward the right-center field stands.

The ball got out there so fast that by the time Lyn Lary looked around, all he saw was outfielder Sam Rice apparently making the catch. Since Lary was already running toward third, he just ran over the base and continued into the Yankees' dugout, thinking the inning was over.

What Lary hadn't seen was the ball rocketing into the stands, where it hit a seat and caromed back onto the field. It was the carom that Rice had caught. Gehrig was circling the bases with his head down. He hadn't seen Lary leave the field and just assumed he had scored ahead of him. Manager Joe McCarthy, third-base coach that day, hadn't seen it either. He had turned his back and was busy cheerleading with the fans.

As soon as Gehrig circled the bases, he was called out for passing Lary and credited with a triple. Larrupin' Lou lost a home run because three people—base runner Lary, manager McCarthy, and Gehrig himself—hadn't been watching the play. When the season ended, Lou and teammate Babe Ruth tied for the home-run lead with forty-six each. Had it not been for one bizarre play, Gehrig would have had forty-seven round trippers and the undisputed homer title.

Chapter 2

It Could Only Happen Once

Some baseball bloopers have happened many times during the game's long history. A key error, a runner being passed on the bases, a collision in the outfield, an easy pop-up dropped at a crucial moment—some of these blunders stand out because of the conditions under which they occurred, but they are all fairly common mishaps.

Other types of foul-ups happen just once. Often these result from a strange bounce of the ball or some other unusual occurrence. The following baseball bloopers are in this category and will probably never happen quite the same way again.

Memories Aren't Made of This

Every big-league player cherishes the memory of his very first at bat in the major leagues. Whether he strikes out or hits a home run, that first appearance represents the culmination of a lifelong dream. Every detail is memorable. But there was one player who remembered only the first half of that historical moment.

He was Billy Herman, a fine hitter who compiled a .304 lifetime batting average during a big-league career that spanned seventeen seasons, from 1931 to 1947. He debuted in the major leagues during the mid–1931 season when the Chicago Cubs called him up from the minors. Herman couldn't wait to join his new teammates and prove himself worthy.

Billy Herman's first-ever major-league at bat for the Cubs in the 1931 season was one he'd never remember. Herman swung hard and fouled the ball straight down at the ground. It bounced up, hit him in the head, and knocked him out cold.

His first at bat came against the Cincinnati Reds and pitcher Si Johnson. Herman could feel the butterflies in his stomach as he stepped to the right side of the plate. He dug in nervously and waited for his pitch. When he got it, he swung from the heels and remembered hearing the crack of the bat as it made contact with the ball. Unfortunately, that sound was all Billy Herman remembered.

He had fouled a Johnson fastball right down to the ground. The ball hit with such force that it bounced up and struck Herman in the back of the head . . . knocking him out cold! Herman—who many years later was inducted into the Hall of Fame—had to be carried from the field on a stretcher. When he woke up in the clubhouse, all he could say was, "What happened?"

More One-of-a-Kind Debuts

While Billy Herman didn't remember his one-of-a-kind first appearance in the major leagues, other players would like to forget theirs. Take the case of Steve Bedrosian, who was brought up by the Atlanta Braves in 1981 and eventually became a fine reliever. Trying to get himself primed and ready for his first ever major-league game, Bedrosian could feel the adrenaline surging. He burst up the dugout steps . . . but never made it to the field. Instead, he ran smack into the dugout railing, not only bruising his arm, but also swallowing the plug of tobacco he had in his mouth. Instead of making a debut to brag about,

Bedrosian spent the entire game sick to his stomach and nursing a painfully bruised arm.

Another let's-try-to-forget-it debut came in 1987 when the Cincinnati Reds called up pitcher Pat Pacillo from Nashville. He was to be the starting pitcher and had to drive four and a half hours from Nashville to reach Riverfront Stadium on time. Stuck in traffic, he didn't arrive at the stadium until after the game had begun.

Already worried about what the Reds would think of his being late, Pacillo then got a nasty surprise. The garage attendant at the ballpark didn't believe that Pacillo was a member of the Reds and refused him entry. With the fans' parking lot full, Pacillo had to park three miles from the stadium and walk back. He didn't arrive until the fourth inning. When he finally got into the game, he gave up two runs in five innings as the Reds lost to the Pirates, 3–2.

Animal Lovers Unite

When Dave Winfield arrived at Toronto's Exhibition Stadium on August 4, 1983, he figured it would be just another day at the ballpark. How wrong he was. Winfield's Yankees were in town to play the Blue Jays, and Big Dave was warming up in the outfield. When it was time to play, the Yankees' outfielder whipped the warmup ball toward the sideline, as he had done so many times over the years. Only this time the ball made an unexpected stop. It

Dave Winfield, shown making a diving catch in the 1981 World Series, was always an impressive outfielder. But before a game in Toronto in 1983, Winfield was tossing a warmup ball off the field when he hit and killed a seagull that had perched on the grass. Believe it or not, Big Dave was briefly charged with animal cruelty.

struck a seagull that had landed in the outfield to look for scraps of food.

Winnie's throw hit the unfortunate bird on the head, killing it instantly. A member of the grounds crew came out and threw a towel over the poor creature before he removed it from the field.

The Toronto crowd suddenly looked upon Winfield as if he were a cold-blooded killer. They began booing and throwing objects at him. Winfield just put his arms out as if to say, "Hey, I didn't do it intentionally." The game continued, but the incident wasn't forgotten.

After the game, Winfield was arrested by the local police and charged with cruelty to animals. He had to post five hundred dollars in bond money so he could leave the city with the team. Suddenly, it looked like he might be in more trouble than if he had bumped an umpire. There was even talk of a jail term.

Fortunately, cooler heads finally prevailed and the charges were dropped. That still didn't stop Yankees manager Billy Martin from taking a playful swipe at his star outfielder.

"Dave couldn't have hit the gull on purpose," Billy the Kid said. "He hasn't hit the cutoff man all year!"

. . . and What Product Is That?

Occasionally, a crazy blooper happens off the diamond—during, for example, public endorsement of products. Many of today's top athletes can pitch products with the skill of a professional actor. In the old days, long before the popularity of television, baseball players got little chance to perfect their off-field presentation skills.

Take the case of that Yankees great Lou Gehrig. A shy man to begin with, Gehrig didn't really like public speaking; nonetheless, he was asked to do a live radio commercial for a popular breakfast cereal called Huskies.

The announcer was to cue Gehrig by asking: "Lou Gehrig, to what do you owe your strength and conditioning?"

All Gehrig had to do was give a one-word answer—Huskies. When the live broadcast took place and the announcer asked the question, Gehrig answered without hesitation.

In a clear voice, he said: "Wheaties!"

The big slugger was more embarrassed than he would have been striking out with the bases loaded. He apologized to the company that made Huskies and said he would refuse any money for the botched commercial. The company's administrators were good sports and paid him anyway, but Gehrig was probably overjoyed to return to the relatively friendly confines of Yankee Stadium.

Not Nose First

Some players make fielding look easy. They are so talented and so relaxed that they make even the tough plays seem routine. Then there are other players who consider every fly ball or pop-up an adventure.

Bill Melton, who played for several American League teams in the late 1960s and 1970s, would never lay claim to having a great glove. A third baseman by trade, Melton stayed in the majors largely because of his bat. When a ball was hit to him in the field, his teammates held their collective breath. At the beginning of the 1970 season,

Melton's fielding was awful—he had committed ten errors in the team's first twenty-four games.

He got worse. During a game in Baltimore on May 7, Melton booted a routine grounder in the third inning for his eleventh error of the season. Three innings later, he really outdid himself. An Oriole batter hit a high pop fly to third. Melton looked up at the ball and camped under it, ready to make the catch. As the ball descended, it hit the heel of his glove, glanced off at full speed, and smashed squarely into his nose.

Melton went down like a shot and remained unconscious for several minutes. He was taken from the field, and a medical examination revealed a broken nose. Not only that, when he reviewed a video of the play, he learned that the official scorer had no choice but to give him another error!

Pine Tar, Anyone?

One of the strangest incidents in baseball history involved a home run that *was* a home run and then *wasn't* a home run—and then, incredibly, was again a home run. The reversals were all because of a substance that was rubbed on a bat. Confused? You should be!

It happened on July 4, 1983, when the Kansas City Royals met the New York Yankees at Yankee Stadium. The Yankees were clinging to a 4–3 lead in the top of the ninth inning and had ace reliever "Goose" Gossage on the mound. With two out and a runner on first, Gossage got set to face the Royals' best hitter, third baseman George Brett. It was a classic confrontation, the flamethrowing Gossage against one of the top hitters in baseball.

Suddenly, Brett jumped on a heater and sent a rocket into the right-field stands for an apparent two-run homer and a 5–4 KC lead. Brett circled the bases with a big smile on his face, but as he crossed home plate, the Yankees' manager, Billy Martin, was already out of the dugout showing home-plate umpire Tim McClelland something on Brett's bat.

Players during that period of baseball history often put a sticky black substance called pine tar on their

Kansas City's George Brett (5) goes berserk after a potential game-winning homer against Yankee relief ace "Goose" Gossage in 1983 was called an out. Why? The umpires ruled that Brett had too much pine tar on his bat. The decision was later reversed and the homer stood.

bats for a better grip. A rule stated that the pine tar could not be more than 18 inches (46 cm) from the knob end of the bat. Martin was claiming the pine tar on Brett's bat extended beyond the limit. Umpire McClelland examined the bat and nodded in agreement. Suddenly, he disallowed the homer and called Brett out!

Brett went berserk and had to be restrained by several teammates as the smug Martin walked back to the dugout. The game ended with an apparent Yankee victory. But that wasn't the end of it. The Royals protested, and American League president Lee MacPhail ruled in their favor. The homer was allowed, and the game would have to be finished with KC ahead, 5–4. MacPhail said that while the pine tar extended farther than the legal limit, it didn't violate "the spirit of the rules."

The contest resumed the next time the two teams met, and the Yanks went down one-two-three in the ninth. The Royals had finally won. Brett's on-again, off-again, on-again homer made the difference. It was something that would never happen again and was, in many ways, a bad joke.

As Yankee outfielder Don Baylor said after he left the field: "If I wanted to watch a soap opera, I'd have turned on the television."

A Windblown Balk

Weather has often played a role in baseball. In northern cities, games have been snowed out early in the year. Late-season games must frequently be completed in damp, rainy weather because there are no more make-up dates. Bad weather can always change the complexion of a game, but perhaps the strangest weather-related incident took place during the 1961 All-Star Game at Candlestick Park in San Francisco.

Candlestick opened in 1960, and it didn't take long for players to realize that bizarre things could happen there. The ballpark was built alongside San Francisco Bay, which has very sudden weather changes.

The 1961 All-Star Game began on a hot afternoon in July. The fans were all in shirtsleeves, and the players quickly broke a sweat on the hot diamond. By the seventh inning, however, the Bay Area's famous winds were beginning to whip up. As Giants reliever Stu Miller entered the game, the gusts were powerful.

Miller was a thin, 165-pound (74-kg) pitcher who was said to throw at three speeds—slow, slower, slowest. As one player remarked, "If you wait five minutes, the ball gets by you fairly fast." But Miller's off-speed pitches kept hitters guessing, and he was a fine relief pitcher for sixteen years.

As Miller got set to face the American Leaguers at Candlestick, the gusts grew stronger and stronger. The game proceeded, and with a runner on first, he got ready to pitch, took the sign from the catcher, and went into his motion.

Just as Miller brought his leg up and his arm back, a powerful 60–mile-per-hour (96-kph) gust of wind bracketed the diamond. Stu Miller was caught in mid-delivery and literally blown off the mound. He had to struggle to keep his feet. Because he had not completed a delivery he started, the umpire had no choice but to call a balk and wave the runner to second. A balk is always a blooper, but this was the first-and-only balk caused by wind.

Miller, by the way, recovered nicely. With the gusts holding off, the gutsy righty struck out Mickey Mantle, Roy Sievers, and Elston Howard in succession—and was the winning pitcher for the National League.

Drop That Pop-Up, or Else!

For pitchers, there is nothing better than getting outs. With each out, the pitcher and his team are one step closer to winning the game. But there was one time when a pitcher didn't want an out—at least not the way he appeared to get it. Not surprisingly, that pitcher was the one-and-only Jay Hanna "Dizzy" Dean.

Diz was not only one of baseball's zaniest characters, a fun-loving country boy who enjoyed practical jokes, he was also one of the game's best pitchers. He won thirty games for the 1934 World Champion St. Louis Cardinals. Unfortunately, a broken toe that he suffered in the 1937 All-Star Game led to arm trouble, which cut short his Hall-of-Fame career. But even today Diz is remembered as much for his unpredictable antics as for his great pitching.

Among other things, Diz loved to brag and to bet. He usually won. One day when Diz was slated to pitch against the Braves in Boston, he bet he would strike out

Vince DiMaggio every time he faced him. Vince was Joe DiMaggio's older brother and not nearly as great a hitter as the famed Yankee Clipper. Sure enough, Diz fanned DiMaggio the first three times he faced him. The fourth time, however, there were two outs in the ninth inning and the tying run on second. Diz would have to whiff DiMaggio again to win his bet.

After two quick strikes, DiMaggio suddenly got his bat on the ball. He lofted a high foul pop behind the plate. The St. Louis catcher circled back, ready to make the catch for the final out of the game. But Dizzy Dean had a look of panic on his face. He didn't want the game to end this way—after all, he'd lose his bet. Suddenly, he began screaming at his catcher, "Drop it! Drop it or you'll never catch me again!"

With Dean screaming like a madman, the startled catcher dropped the ball. Cards manager Frank Frisch was so angered by Dean's actions that he jumped up to pull him out of the game. But he jumped so hard that he slammed his head on the top of the dugout; dazed, he had to sit back down. That gave Diz a chance to throw another blazing fastball, which he "fogged" past DiMaggio for strike three and the final out.

Now Diz was happy. He had won the game and made good on his boast. To do it, he forced his catcher to commit a blooper that might have cost the Cards the game. But the outcome was never in doubt for the supremely confident Dean. And how much did Dean win on his bet? Eighty cents!

Chapter 3

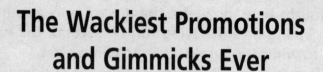

The Wackiest Promotions and Gimmicks Ever

Baseball has always been, first and foremost, a competitive sport. The object is to win, with the World Series the ultimate goal. But baseball is also a game, and games should be fun. Over the years, many owners have tried to make baseball even more fun for the fans by holding special events and promotions. Giveaways, such as bat day, cap day, and shirt day, always bring extra fans to the ballparks. Occasionally, however, strange promotions and gimmicks backfire to the point of being ridiculous. Some have even been dangerous to the fans and players alike. Perhaps there aren't as many of these in the 1990s because owners are a bit more careful than they used to be and can make money from skyboxes and season tickets. But in previous decades, special promotions were always eagerly awaited—sometimes with questionable results.

A Bonfire Between Games

A promo featuring a bonfire was devised by White Sox owner Bill Veeck, often a master at drawing fans to the ballpark. It backfired in more ways than one on July 12, 1979, at Comiskey Park in Chicago. One of the big fads at that time was disco music, a particular style Veeck didn't like. So he got together with a Chicago disc jockey to give rock-and-roll fans a chance to demonstrate against disco.

Veeck announced that, between games of a doubleheader in which the White Sox would meet the Detroit Tigers, a bonfire would be built in center field. Fans could demonstrate by burning all the disco records they could bring to the ballpark. Admission would be just ninety-eight cents. When more than fifty thousand fans came through the turnstiles, Veeck thought his promotion was a success. How wrong he was.

After just a few innings of the first game, fans holding their records had a bright idea. When thrown, a 45 rpm record would behave just like a Frisbee. Guess what? Records began sailing through the air and onto the field. The game had to be stopped several times so the mess could be cleaned up. That opened the floodgates. Fans soon were throwing other things, like firecrackers and golf balls, one of which almost hit Tigers center fielder Ron LeFlore.

Finally the first game ended, and it was time for the bonfire. Once the fire was lit, the fans went nuts. Some seven thousand of them poured from the stands

A crazy promotion gimmick gone wrong. Fans are shown here overrunning Comiskey Park in Chicago on July 12, 1979, between games of a doubleheader. There was supposed to be an anti-disco music demonstration, with records burned in a bonfire. The fans became so unruly that the second game couldn't be played and had to be forfeited.

and ran wild all over the field. Veeck even got on the P.A. to try to clear the field. Finally, helmeted police had to be called in. More than fifty people were arrested, and several had to be treated for injuries.

The whole promotion had literally gone up in smoke. The field was in such bad shape that the second game couldn't begin. The next day it was forfeited to Detroit. Some called it Disco Demolition Night. For master promoter Bill Veeck, it may have been the biggest promotional blooper of his life.

40

Coming up for Air

Not all of baseball's crazy promotions happen in the major leagues. The minor leagues have always tried to promote their teams to keep the fans coming. Stan Wasiak, who was the longtime manager of the Los Angeles Dodgers' minor-league team in Vero Beach, Florida, remembers a couple of real wild ones.

There was the time a guy walked up to the owner of a minor-league team in Grand Rapids, Michigan, and said he had an act the fans would love. He wanted to be buried alive in a box behind home plate while the entire game was being played. He told the owner he did it for a living and there was nothing to worry about.

"Before the game they dug a hole behind home plate, put the box down, and he got into it," Wasiak remembered. "Then they covered the hole with dirt and said, 'Play ball!'"

A nine-inning baseball game took place, but no one in the park, fans and players alike, could stop thinking about the guy in the box. When the game ended, not a single person left the park. Everyone waited to see the grounds crew dig up the box. As the onlookers held their breaths, the man emerged, groggy but otherwise fine.

"He told us later that he had enough air for between two and a half and three hours," Wasiak recalled. "I couldn't help wondering what would have happened if the game had gone into extra innings."

That strange promotion was considered a success.

Really, What Is a Reggie Bar?

Many of baseball's offbeat promotions are staged by teams with losing records who are also losing fans. Bring on a wild promo and bring the fans back—that's the theory. But sometimes winning teams' promotions turn out to be real bloopers.

In 1978, the world-champion New York Yankees fell into the promo trap. The year before, the Yanks had won the World Series from the L.A. Dodgers, largely on the strength of Reggie Jackson's five homers—the last three coming in the final game. During the off-season, Reggie remarked to someone that he should have a candy bar named for himself. A short time later the Reggie Bar was born, a circular-shaped chocolate-covered candy with a colorful wrapper. It's creation gave Yankees management an idea.

For the home opener against the White Sox in 1978, each paying customer was given a free Reggie Bar. Some 44,667 fans filed into Yankee Stadium on April 13, but a candy bar, unlike a free bat or T-shirt, isn't a keeper. When the real Reggie came up in the first inning and blasted a three-run homer, the jubilant home fans celebrated by flinging their Reggie Bars onto the field.

That started it. For the rest of the game, Reggie Bars flew through the stands and onto the field. The grounds crew must have picked up thousands of the uneaten candies, and they almost cost the Yankees a forfeit. When the Yanks finally won the game, 4–2, Sox manager Bob Lemon grumped about the Reggie Bar.

"How great a tasting candy bar could it be if they throw it instead of eat it?" Lemon quipped.

We're Being Bombed

The Atlanta Braves management thought they were being quite patriotic when they announced that there would be a big fireworks display at Atlanta's Fulton County Stadium after the game on July 4, 1985. The Braves were hosting the New York Mets that night, and some 44,947 fans turned out to watch the game and then celebrate the glorious fourth.

Things soon began to go wrong. Before the game even started, there was an eighty-four-minute rain delay. Then, during the third inning, a forty-one-minute interruption stalled the game. Thus an additional two hours were tagged onto game time. Moreover, the game itself turned into a slugfest that was tied at the end of nine innings. Neither team could score again as the extra innings rolled on. Slowly, the fans began leaving as the hours passed. As the early morning of July 5 rolled around, the game continued.

Mercifully, after nineteen innings of play, the Mets took a 16–13 victory to end the marathon. It was 3:55 A.M. when the game ended. It had lasted six hours and ten minutes. Tack on the rain delay, and you had the latest finish of a game in league history. Approximately eight thousand fans were there when the last out was finally recorded. But wait, what about the big fireworks display?

Not wanting to go back on its promise to the fans, management arranged for the "bombs" to go off at 4:01 A.M. At least that's what it sounded like to those already sleeping in the vicinity of the stadium, and it created a real panic. People leaped out of bed thinking the city was under attack. One person living near the ballpark called 911 and screamed, "We're being bombed!"

A staff member of the Atlanta Public Safety Department put it this way: "There were a few minutes when we thought we had a mini-panic on our hands. The first thing we heard was this huge explosion that must have knocked everyone out of bed. People were running out into the streets, some were rushing to the precinct office, and others were jamming our phone lines. Most of the neighborhood thought the Civil War had started all over again."

This was an innocent, safety-conscious promotion based on good intentions. Bad weather and an extra-inning game turned it into a blooper. Officials erred when they didn't call the fireworks off and reschedule them for another night.

And Now Batting . . . Eddie Gaedel

Along with ill-conceived promotions that have backfired over the years, baseball has also been the home to many strange gimmicks, used either to hype the game or simply to gain an advantage over an opponent. None is better remembered than the one engineered by Bill Veeck when he owned the old St.

44

Louis Browns in 1951. The Browns were floundering in last place as usual, and Veeck decided to create a little excitement.

The Browns were hosting the Detroit Tigers for a Sunday doubleheader in late August. The first game was uneventful. Then, in the nightcap, the Browns came to bat at the bottom of the first inning. Frank Saucier was due to lead off against the Tigers' Bob Cain. Suddenly, a pinch hitter was announced, and the fans couldn't believe their eyes. It looked as if the Browns were sending a little boy up to the plate.

Three-foot, seven-inch (1.09-m) Eddie Gaedel pinch hit for the St. Louis Browns in a 1951 game against Detroit. Gaedel drew a walk from pitcher Bob Cain. Though Browns' owner Bill Veeck had signed Gaedel to a legal contract, the American League ruled against letting him play again.

Pitcher Cain looked down at a batter who was just 3 feet, 7 inches (1.09 m) tall and weighed 65 pounds (29 kg). He had the number $\frac{1}{8}$ on his uniform. Umpire Ed Hurley called time and demanded to know what was going on. The Browns' manager, Zack Taylor, came out of the dugout and showed Hurley a legal major-league contract. It identified the batter as twenty-six-year-old Eddie Gaedel, who happened to be a midget. With the contract legal and Gaedel an adult, Hurley had no choice but to let him hit as the fans cackled with glee.

Gaedel got into the batter's box and went into a deep crouch. Not surprisingly, pitcher Cain couldn't find the tiny strike zone, and Gaedel walked on four pitches. The Browns then sent a pinch runner to take his place. No one will ever know whether Veeck intended to use Gaedel in the future when his team needed a walk. The next day the American League president, Will Harridge, announced he would not approve Gaedel's contract, that his signing by Veeck was considered "conduct detrimental to baseball."

As for Eddie Gaedel, who is officially credited with a single at bat in the major leagues, it was an experience he would never forget.

"I felt like Babe Ruth when I walked out on the field that day," he declared proudly.

A New Group of Managers

Bill Veeck had to be one of the most fun-loving owners in baseball history. He always tried to entertain the fans, even when his teams were big losers. Just five days after sending little Eddie Gaedel up as a pinch hitter for his St. Louis Browns in 1951, Veeck was at it again. He announced that there would be another promotion. This time some one thousand fans would be allowed to manage his team for one game.

Sounds amazing, right? Here's what happened. When the Browns met the Philadelphia Athletics on August 24, a group of 1,115 fans sitting behind the Browns' dugout where given "yes" and "no" cards. Whenever a managerial decision arose during the game, the fans were asked to flash the cards, yes or no, to make the decision. Their decision, the Browns' management said, would be final.

In fact, they even got to pick the lineup. Their first decision was to bench catcher Matt Batts and first baseman Ben Taylor in favor of Sherm Lollar and Hank Arft. Lollar got three hits and two RBIs, while Arft also drove in two runs. And when St. Louis starter Ned Garver allowed hits to five of the first six A's batters, the fan/managers were asked if a relief pitcher should warm up. They voted no. Garver then went on to allow only two hits the rest of the way in a 5–3 St. Louis win.

Believe it or not, the fans made all the right decisions. So where's the blooper? Maybe it was that Bill Veeck's promotion showed that managers could be excess baggage. Just let the fans decide. Of course, it might have been plain old dumb luck. Either way, Veeck never ran that promotion again.

Dig Those Crazy Legs

Over the years, baseball teams have occasionally worn some bizarre uniforms. These outfits were gimmicks thought up to make a team look sharper, but they usually ended up making the players look silly. In 1916, for example, the Brooklyn Dodgers took the field in checkered uniforms. They were trying to compete with the crosstown Yankees, who had donned pinstripes the previous year. Even the Dodger players seemed embarrassed by the checkered shirts and pants. They made the players look like walking tic-tac-toe games. The new uniforms were quickly discarded.

By the 1970s, uniforms had been pretty much standard for years. The home team wore white, and the visitors gray. In the early 1970s, the Oakland A's began wearing colored uniforms. The first were green and gold. Done tastefully, it worked, and many teams went on to use other colors. One owner, however, took it too far in 1976. Guess which one? Bill Veeck, of course.

On August 8, Veeck's Chicago White Sox took the field wearing white shirts with blue lettering. Nothing wrong with that. But below the shirts the Sox players were wearing navy blue shorts! It was the first time ever that a major-league club had worn shorts, and the gimmick was a complete bust.

The players on the opposing team that day, the Kansas City Royals, collapsed in laughter as soon as they saw the shorts. They began ribbing the Sox players mercilessly. The White Sox won the ball game but lost the fashion show. The shorts didn't pass muster with anyone. Besides, they offered little protection for players sliding into bases or diving for balls in the field. Too easy to get cuts, bruises, and road rash. The shorts, like most gimmicks, were a short-lived blooper.

Chapter 4

The Worst Trades and Deals Ever Made

Trades and other deals have always been a big part of sports, although free agency has changed the rules markedly in recent years. Veteran players are now free to leave their teams when certain conditions are met. If a team feels it is going to lose a player, it is sometimes forced to make a trade first. In the old days, however, players were bound to their teams for life—unless they were traded or released. A perfect trade is one that benefits both teams, but that doesn't happen too often. Some trades are bad risks from the start: A team may be hoping that a veteran player can coax out one or two more good years, or that a young player will realize his unfulfilled potential. Other deals go bad if a player is suddenly injured. Some trades are just a joke from the start—bloopers that leave one team laughing and the other licking its wounds. Let's take a look at some of the sorriest trades and deals in baseball history.

That's Showbiz

Imagine a team getting rid of arguably the best player in baseball so the team owner can finance a Broadway show! Believe it or not, it really happened. It's a story that still eats at the hearts of Boston Red Sox fans everywhere.

George Herman Ruth joined the Red Sox late in the 1914 season. He was a big left-handed pitcher with plenty of promise. During the next three years he won sixty-five games and looked like an up-and-coming superstar on the mound. But Ruth was doing more than pitching; he could also hit the ball farther than anyone else in the league.

Ruth helped the Red Sox win the World Series in 1917 and again in 1918. By 1919, he went just 9–5 on the mound. That's because he was setting a new batting record with 29 home runs, driving in 114 runs, and hitting .322. He had been great as a pitcher and now was great as a hitter. Ruth was already the most valuable commodity in baseball.

That's when the Red Sox pulled the biggest blooper of all time. On January 20, 1920, Red Sox management shocked the baseball world by announcing that George Herman Ruth had been sold to the New York Yankees for the then enormous sum of $125,000. That's all the Bosox got in return. Cash. No players. It seems that Red Sox owner Harry Frazee's real love was show business. Frazee needed money for his latest production, and the fastest way to get it was to sell his star player.

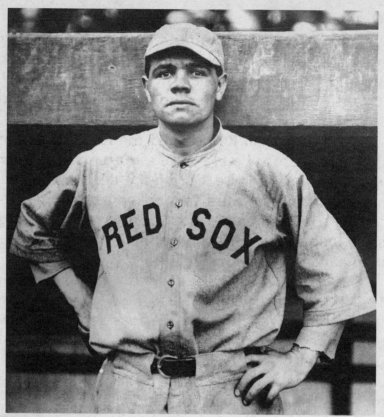

This slim youngster is the one-and-only Babe Ruth in his early years as a Red Sox pitcher. The man who would become the game's greatest slugger and gate attraction was sold to the New York Yankees for $125,000 prior to the 1920 season because Boston owner Harry Frazee needed money to put on a Broadway show.

As for Ruth, he quickly became a full-time outfielder and blasted an unheard-of 54 homers his first year as a Yankee. As "Babe" Ruth, he would smash 714 home runs during his career and help make the Yankees the most feared team in baseball.

Nicknamed "the Bambino" and "the Sultan of Swat," he was not only the greatest player of his time, but also one of the most charismatic players ever.

Harry Frazee is still a villain in Boston. He was never a rousing success in the theater, and he lived to see the Babe hit 60 home runs in 1927. Frazee died in 1929, but his blooper of a deal will live forever.

Trading an Express for a Local

In the New York Mets' early years, the team always had problems finding a third baseman. The Mets were an expansion team in 1962, but with a brace of good young pitchers, they surprised everyone by winning the World Series in 1969. Despite their sudden success, they still didn't have the player they wanted at third. After winning the Series in 1969, the Mets traded promising outfielder Amos Otis to the Kansas City Royals for a young third baseman named Joe Foy. Mistake number one.

Otis became a star in KC, one of the better all-around outfielders in the league. Foy was a complete bust. He played one year in New York, was traded again, played one more season, then was out of baseball. So the Mets started shopping again, and their second deal for a third baseman was worse than the first.

Following the 1971 season, the Mets announced they had traded an erratic young fastball pitcher named Nolan Ryan to the California Angels for veteran shortstop Jim Fregosi, who would shift to third base for the Mets. Ryan was a strikeout pitcher whose wildness kept him from joining the regular Mets rotation. Fregosi had been an American League all-star on more than one occasion. This time the Mets thought they had made a smart move. They were wrong.

Fregosi was over-the-hill. He played two dismal years for the Mets before moving on, his playing days all but done. As for Ryan, he became a legend, one of the most dynamic pitchers in baseball history. He not only threw his incredible fastball well into his forties, but was also the author of a record-setting seven no-hitters. Plus, he retired as baseball's all-time strikeout leader with more than five thousand whiffs.

He was known as the Ryan Express for his blazing fastball, but the Mets wound up trading him for a "local." Like all trades that backfire, it seemed like a good idea at the time.

A 246-Game Winner for a College Kid

Talk about a one-sided trade, one that happened one hundred years ago takes the cake. During the 1890s, the New York Giants had a right-handed pitcher named Amos Rusie. From 1890 to 1898, Rusie won more than 20 games every year—and four of those years he won more than 30 games. In fact, he had already won 234 games before he sat out the 1896 season because of a contract dispute (yes, they even had contract disputes in the early days of baseball). He was one of the greatest pitchers of his era.

But Rusie had been feuding with the Giants' owner, Andrew Freedman, ever since sitting out the 1896 season. In 1898, Rusie injured his arm while picking off a runner at first and sat out the next year. At that point, the Giants were eyeing a young pitcher from Bucknell University named Christy Mathewson. The New Yorkers feared that Cincinnati might put in a claim for Mathewson and sign him. To make sure that didn't happen, they decided to trade Rusie and his 246 lifetime wins for the right to sign Mathewson.

The Reds decided to gamble on the trade. After all, there was no guarantee that a college kid would make the grade in a tough business. Since Rusie himself was still young—just twenty-eight years old—Cincy officials expected him to regain his winning form. It didn't happen. Rusie couldn't pitch at all in 1899. He tried a brief comeback in 1901, failed to win a game, and retired.

As for Christy Mathewson, he went on to become one of the greatest pitchers in baseball history, winning 373 games and a place of honor in diamond annals. Today, both Mathewson and Rusie are in the Hall of Fame, but that didn't help Cincinnati. They traded for a great pitcher—but one who didn't win a single game for them. In turn, they gave up the rights to a hurler who would win 373 and become a legend.

The Cincinnati Reds not only traded away Christy Mathewson but also made another trade blooper more than half a century later. Slugger Frank Robinson had been a Reds mainstay since winning the Rookie of the Year Award in 1956. In 1961, when the Reds won the National League pennant, Robby was the league's Most Valuable Player, compiling a .323 batting average, 37 homers, and 124 RBIs. A year later, Robinson hit .342, with 39 homers and 136 runs batted in. He had surely become one of baseball's great players.

By 1965, Robinson's numbers were down only slightly. He still batted .296, and had 33 homers and 113 RBIs. Just thirty years old, Robinson appeared— to everyone but the Cincinnati Reds—to be in the prime of his baseball career. So on December 9, the Reds shocked everyone by announcing that Robinson had been traded to the Baltimore Orioles for pitcher Milt Pappas.

The Reds defended their incomprehensible move by saying they felt Robinson was "an old thirty," a player already on the downslide. Pappas was a solid, though not spectacular, pitcher who usually won between twelve and sixteen games a season. Trading a superstar for a good, not great, pitcher—it just didn't seem right, and it wasn't.

In his first year with the Orioles, Robinson won the American League Triple Crown with a batting average of .316, 49 homers, and 129 RBIs. He also

Hall of Famer Frank Robinson slides back into first during a game against Cleveland. Robby was traded to the Orioles by the Reds in 1966 because he was supposedly an "old thirty." What a blooper. Robinson won the A.L. Triple Crown in 1966 and led the O's to four World Series appearances.

led his team to a World Series triumph. He continued his outstanding career, both as a player and inspirational leader, and helped the Orioles into the World Series three more times. He finished his career with 586 home runs, fourth on the all-time list. Of those homers, 262 came after his trade. As for Pappas, he was just 30–29 in two-plus seasons with Cincinnati, before getting traded again.

A Bat and Legs for a Bum Arm

Similar to the Robinson-Pappas trade was the one between the Chicago Cubs and the St. Louis Cardinals in the middle of the 1964 season. The Cubs had a young outfielder named Lou Brock, who had hit just

.263 and .268 his first two years with the team. Some fifty games into the 1964 season, Brock was again hovering around the .250 mark. The Cubs' brain trust felt he was a player who wasn't going to make it big.

They decided to make a trade with the Cards, who were offering pitcher Ernie Broglio. He had won twenty-one games in 1960 and another eighteen in 1963. Though Broglio was just 3–5 at the time of the trade, the Cubs felt he could regain the form of a big winner. The deal was made. Oops!

Brock hit .348 for the remainder of the season and helped the Cardinals win the pennant and the World Series. From there, he put together a Hall of Fame career that included more than three thousand hits. He retired as baseball's all-time stolen-base king for career (938) and year (118), though both those marks have since been broken by Rickey Henderson. Brock also helped his team into another pair of World Series and was one of the most exciting players of his time.

As for Broglio, he never regained his winning form. A series of arm problems led to his premature retirement several years after the trade was made. The Cubs traded a future Hall of Famer and got virtually nothing in return.

The Strangest Deals Ever

There have been all kinds of player trades over the years. Not all of them were straight-up, one-for-one deals. Some have been two or three for one, five for two, and other multi-player transactions. In the early days of the game, players weren't even necessarily traded for other players!

Most baseball fans know the name Cy Young. Every year the best pitcher in each league is given the Cy Young Award. That's because Young was the winningest pitcher in baseball history, with 511 victories. However, early in his career, Young was involved in one of baseball's strangest trades. He was a little-known rookie pitching for Canton of the Tri-State League in 1889. The old Cleveland team in the National League wanted Young for the 1890 season, so they made a deal. They bought future Hall of Famer Cy Young from Canton for—get this—a suit of clothes!

Another hard-to-believe deal involved a Hall of Fame pitcher named Robert "Lefty" Grove, who was toiling in the minor leagues in 1920 as pitcher for a team in Martinsburg, West Virginia. The old Baltimore Orioles, also a minor-league team back then, wanted Grove. Jack Dunn, owner of the Orioles, found a very creative way to get him. Dunn learned that the Martinsburg team still owed money to the contractors who put up the outfield fence at their stadium. So when he asked for Grove, he offered to put up the money to pay for the fence!

After four years in Baltimore, Grove joined the Philadelphia Athletics to begin a big-league career that would see him win three hundred games. Who knows where he would have ended up if the outfield fence in Martinsburg had already been paid for.

Seems like the early days of the game were filled with trades that would be absolutely ridiculous today. In 1905, for example, the Detroit Tigers were cornered into a peculiar deal. The team conducted spring training in Augusta, Georgia, but when it was time to break camp and head north, they didn't have enough money to pay for the use of the Augusta facilities. The front office came up with a quick solution. Several weeks later, in return for the rent money, Detroit gave the Augusta minor-league team a young pitcher named Eddie Cicotte, who had a 1–1 record for the Tigers in the early season. At the time, it seemed a small price to pay.

Cicotte surfaced with Boston three years later and eventually went to the Chicago White Sox, where in 1920 he was one of eight players banned from baseball for life. They were charged with conspiring with gamblers to throw the 1919 World Series. Cicotte, however, was also an outstanding pitcher who won 208 games before being banned. Had Detroit not decided to use him to pay the rent, his big-league career might have taken a different turn. He might never have become a member of that infamous group.

Chapter 5

Things They'd Rather Forget

In baseball, as in other sports, there is always a winner and a loser. Winning obviously brings greater joy and satisfaction than losing, which for most athletes is very hard to take. The only gratification found in losing is knowing that you gave the game your absolute best. Sometimes, however, the memory of losing lingers. Maybe the failure happened at a big game, a dramatic moment in a game, or even throughout an entire season—then it's hard to forget it. Or a team could have a long losing streak, a particularly one-sided loss, or the inability to come up big in certain situations. Occasionally there is a downright blooper—something everybody knows shouldn't have happened. Such moments are better forgotten, but their memory seems impossible to shake.

Here's a group of famous and not-so-famous baseball happenings that those involved wish could be forgotten—forever.

In 1940, the Brooklyn Dodgers brought up a twenty-one-year-old rookie outfielder named Pete Reiser. Pistol Pete, as he was called, had all the tools to be a great player. He began proving it a year later when he led the National League in hitting with a .343 average. The year after that he seemed ready to attain superstar status. By July 1942, he was leading the league in hitting, with an average climbing above the .380 mark. Many felt he had the talent to hit .400. Only then did Pete Reiser run into the one foe he couldn't overcome . . . outfield fences.

For some reason, the reckless Reiser couldn't stop himself when going after a fly ball. His first collision with an immovable fence happened that July in St. Louis, and it ruined his season. He returned to action a short time later, but he'd lost his edge and wound up hitting .310. Unfortunately, that wasn't the end of it.

Reiser just kept running into walls, which weren't padded back then, even after ballparks began installing warning tracks to make outfielders more wary. Reiser hit just .277 the following year and was no more than a part-time player until he retired in 1952. Outfield fences were his recurring nightmare. His frequent collisions resulted in several concussions, two broken ankles, a broken right elbow, and severe injuries to his left knee and left leg.

It was a case of unrealized potential. As his manager at Brooklyn, Leo Durocher, put it: "Pete

Reiser might have been the best baseball player I ever saw. He was a switch hitter, had power from both sides, could run fast and throw well. He had everything but luck."

A Real Case of Hot-Dogging

Here's one that will make you laugh, but the player involved probably wished it hadn't happened. Gates Brown was a burly 220-pounder (82 kg) and a slashing hitter for the Detroit Tigers in the 1960s and early 1970s. Brown, however, wasn't real fast and was just a mediocre outfielder. As a result, he spent a good part of his career as a pinch hitter.

Brown loved to eat almost as much as he loved to play baseball. On August 7, 1968, the Tigers were playing the Cleveland Indians. As usual, Brown was on the bench. By the sixth inning he was getting hungry, so he sneaked out of the dugout and went into the clubhouse to grab a snack. He got himself two hot dogs, covered them with mustard and ketchup, and returned to the dugout.

He figured he could munch on the hot dogs in the corner and no one would notice because his pinch hitting appearances usually took place later in the game. He had just bitten into the first hot dog when he heard manager Mayo Smith hollering at him to get a bat and pinch hit.

Brown, besides holding a hot dog in each hand, had his belt unbuckled and his shoes untied. He knew he had to get ready fast. So he stuffed the hot dogs inside his uniform jersey, then tied his shoes and buckled his belt. The warm wieners were still tucked inside his jersey when he came up to hit.

"I always wanted to get a hit every time I went up to the plate," Brown said later. "But this was one time I didn't want a hit. Wouldn't you know it, I smacked one in the gap and had to slide into second base headfirst."

Brown got his double, all right, but he also got something else. When he stood up, mustard and ketchup were smeared all over his jersey, with the remnants of the hot dogs and buns falling out. The Cleveland fielders saw him and began laughing, as did his teammates on the bench.

"It had to be my most embarrassing moment in baseball," Brown confided.

Manager Smith, probably holding back a laugh, fined Brown $100 for breaking a rule that forbade eating on the bench. By the time Smith asked Brown why he had done it, Brown had recovered his sense of humor.

The player explained that he was hungry. "Besides," he added, "where else can you eat a hot dog and have the best seat in the house?"

Hit the Guy!

In 1942, the Boston Braves brought up a rookie left-hander named Warren Spahn. Casey Stengel was the manager at the time, and the Braves weren't very good. Spahn was pitching in his fourth game, against the Dodgers on April 20, when Stengel got mad. He thought the Dodgers were stealing signs, and he wanted to send a message. So he told Spahn to hit the next Dodger hitter, Pee Wee Reese.

The young lefty wasn't used to this kind of big-league strategy. His first pitch sailed behind Reese, who knew what was happening and just laughed. Again Stengel gave Spahn the signal to hit Reese. This time he aimed for Pee Wee's chin and missed.

Twice more he tried and missed, as Reese drew a walk. Later, Spahn heard it from his manager.

"He cursed me out," Spahnnie remembered. "He said I had to learn better control if I ever expected to make it in the majors. Believe me, I threw all sorts of balls at Pee Wee, but I just couldn't hit him."

The next day Spahn got his punishment. He was returned to the minor-league team in Hartford—just because he couldn't hit a batter, something he always tried to forget. Fortunately, the incident didn't deter Spahn. After spending three years in military service during World War II, he returned to the Braves and became the winningest left-hander in history, with 363 victories in his long career. Never again would he be punished for failing to hit someone. He was simply too good.

Wait, That Wasn't the Signal!

When is a signal not a signal? When the manager has a cold. Here's a strange case of the signal that wasn't, and it cost the Cleveland Indians a ball game.

It happened in 1942, the first year that shortstop Lou Boudreau was the player/manager of the Indians. During one series of games, Boudreau came down with a bad head cold. He took himself out of the lineup, but as manager he flashed the signals from the dugout to his third-base coach.

The signal for the rarely used double steal was the manager putting a towel to his face. At one point in the game, the Indians had runners on first and second. Both were slow, especially Pat Seerey at second. No one in his right mind would ask those two guys to try a double steal. But when third-base coach Oscar Melillo looked into the dugout, he saw Boudreau with a towel to his face. The signal was unmistakable, and Melillo flashed it to the surprised runners.

Sure enough, simultaneous with the pitch, the two runners plodded off their bases. They were both cut down for a double play. When Melillo returned to the dugout, Boudreau exploded, demanding to know why his coach had signaled such a stupid play. Melillo explained where he had gotten the signal.

Then the manager remembered. His head cold was so bad that, without thinking, he had grabbed a towel to blow his nose—and inadvertently given the signal for the double steal. While blowing his nose, he also blew the game.

Can't Anyone Here Start a Rally?

Here's one that every player on the winning team would always remember, while every player on the losing team would give anything to forget. It was a game between the Boston Red Sox and the St. Louis Browns at Fenway Park, Boston, on June 8, 1950. The Sox had a powerhouse hitting team featuring Ted Williams, Bobby Doerr, Walt Dropo, Vern Stephens, Dom DiMaggio, and Billy Goodman. They were battling for the American League pennant. The Browns, as usual, were battling to stay out of the basement. The previous day, the Red Sox had really unloaded on St. Louis pitching, winning by the unlikely and embarrassing score of 20–4, one of the worst beatings ever. It couldn't possibly happen that way again.

For one inning it didn't. Boston's Chuck Stobbs and the Browns' Cliff Fannin matched goose eggs in the first. Would it be a pitcher's battle? No such luck. After Stobbs retired the Brownies in the top of the second, the Boston bats exploded. They scored eight runs in the second, five in the third, and seven more in the fourth. After only four innings, Boston had a 20–3 lead, and they weren't finished yet. By the end of the game, the Bosox had battered four St. Louis pitchers for twenty-eight hits and a 29–4 victory. It was the most one-sided victory in baseball history.

The Browns players must have had nightmares for weeks. The Sox banged out nine doubles, a triple, and seven home runs on their way to setting a record of sixty total bases for the game. After losing 20–4, the Browns lost 29–4. Talk about being shellshocked!

A Dropped Third Strike for the Ages

This is a classic blooper that will live on in baseball history—the most famous dropped third strike in baseball annals. But was it really the catcher's fault?

In the 1941 World Series, between the Brooklyn Dodgers and New York Yankees, the powerful Yanks were heavy favorites, but the scrappy Dodgers were fighting all the way. The teams split the first two games at Yankee Stadium, then the Bronx Bombers won the third at Ebbets Field to take a 2–1 lead. In the crucial fourth game, the Dodgers held a 4–3 lead going into the ninth inning. If they could hang on, they would tie the series at two games each and have a good chance to win.

Dodger reliever Hugh Casey looked as if he really had it going. He was in his fourth inning of work and had shut the door on the Yankee bats. He got the first two men in the ninth and only had to retire Tommy Henrich to end the game. The count went to 3–2. What the next pitch was is a mystery to this day. It broke down and in as Henrich swung . . . and missed. A roar went up from the Dodger crowd as Henrich started to walk back to the bench. It seemed as if the game was over.

But wait a minute! Suddenly, Dodger catcher Mickey Owen whirled around. The pitch had skipped off the tip of his glove and was rolling to the backstop. On a dropped third strike, the batter can run to first. That's just what Henrich did, and he was safe. The game wasn't over. Owen, it appeared, had committed a huge blooper.

Now the Yanks had new life, and they made the most of it. Joe DiMaggio was up next and singled. Then Charley Keller whacked a double. The rattled Casey then walked Bill Dickey, followed by another double by Joe Gordon. By the time he got the third out, Hugh Casey had given up four runs. The Yanks went on to win, 7–4. The next day they closed out the Series in five games.

Who was the goat? For years, people assumed it was catcher Owen, who failed to catch a sharp-breaking curve. But pitcher Casey was known to throw an illegal spitter occasionally, and therein lies the mystery. Did Hugh Casey throw a spitball, which can dip and dive in erratic ways? If he did, was Mickey Owen ready for it? Some say yes, some say no. Either way, it was a blooper that enabled the Yankees to win an important game—one that they probably should have lost.

You've Got to Touch Second

It was a simple error of omission, but it cost the New York Giants the National League pennant. Who should really take the blame? The jury's still out on this one.

Let's set the scene. The New York Giants and Chicago Cubs were locked in a tight pennant race the final week of the 1908 season. On September 23, the two teams met for an important game in New

York. It was a pitcher's battle, tied at 1–1 in the bottom of the ninth. Then the Giants rallied. With two outs, the Giants had Moose McCormick on second and nineteen-year-old Fred Merkle on first.

Al Bridwell was up. He picked out his pitch and lined a hit to center field. McCormick sped home with what appeared to be the winning run. Now things get confusing. Young Merkle, upon seeing the winning run crossing the plate, stopped running just before he touched second base, turned, and started toward the clubhouse. It was common practice in those days for players to stop as soon as the winning run scored. Technically, however, it was a violation of a rule that said a player had to touch base—in this case, second—to complete the play. Only it was a rule that was never enforced back then.

But with so much at stake, it was time to honor the rule. Cubs second baseman Johnny Evers saw what happened and began screaming for the ball. At this point, the ballpark was in chaos. Thinking the Giants had won, the fans came streaming onto the field to celebrate. Some say the Giants' Joe McGinnity got his hands on the ball and tossed it into the stands. Then another ball was thrown onto the field from the Cubs' dugout and relayed to Evers, who touched second and appealed to umpire Hank O'Day to call Merkle out. O'Day had no choice but to enforce the rule that had so often been ignored. He called Merkle out, negating the run.

A wild scene followed, players and fans going

berserk. Did Evers have an illegal ball? What would the decision have been if the original ball was thrown in the stands by McGinnity? With the fans swarming the field, the game couldn't continue. It was ruled a tie. When the two teams finished the year with identical 98–55 records, the controversial tie game had to be replayed. This time, the Cubs won, 4–2, and claimed the pennant.

In the eyes of most baseball fans, nineteen-year-old Merkle had committed the all-time bonehead play. Although Merkle went on to have a long and fine career, he never escaped the tag "Bonehead"; it haunted him the rest of his life.

Perhaps it was Giants' manager John McGraw who put it all into perspective. A tough-as-nails leader, McGraw never blamed Merkle.

"[Merkle] did not cost us the pennant," McGraw said. "We lost a dozen games we should have won, and any one of them could have saved the pennant for us."

That was undoubtedly true, but in baseball lore, "Bonehead" Merkle made the blooper that "cost" the Giants the crown.

Hey, Diz, It's Only a Game

Without a doubt, Dizzy Dean was one of the most outrageous characters ever to play baseball. He was happy-go-lucky, riding fire engines and throwing water balloons out hotel windows. On the mound, however, he was a fierce competitor who hated to lose—and he didn't like hitters. He loved to brag about striking them out with his live fastball, which he always said he "fogged" past them.

But not even Diz was on his game all the time. During spring training in 1934, a year in which he would win thirty games, Diz's temper flared in a way even he would probably have liked to forget. The Cardinals were in Miami, Florida, playing a pre-season exhibition game against the Giants. Diz didn't have it that day. The Giants touched him up for seven runs in a single inning. When he went out for the next inning, Diz was rip-roaring mad.

The one-and-only Dizzy Dean "fogging" another fastball toward home plate. One of baseball's all-time zaniest characters, Diz once hit seven straight Giants' batters in an exhibition game because he had given up seven runs and was mad.

When the first batter stepped in, Diz promptly plunked him with a fastball. Then the next Giant hitter came up. Diz plunked him. Then he hit the next with another well-placed heater. It was apparent that Dean wasn't going to give anyone a chance to swing the bat. He hit seven batters in a row, giving the Giants four more runs. Diz didn't care; he thought he was sending a message the Giants wouldn't forget, and no one could stop him.

Finally, the plate umpire appealed to the Cards' manager, Frankie Frisch. "Get that maniac off the mound," he barked. Frisch complied, and Dizzy laughed all the way to the clubhouse.

If a pitcher tried that today he would be fined, and both benches would empty in an all-out brawl. Dizzy Dean got away with it.

A Blooper Brawl If There Ever Was One

In April 1979, the two-time defending world champion New York Yankees were off to another good start, leading the American League's Eastern Division. Many felt the Yanks, with a powerful lineup and a solid starting rotation, were a good bet to make it three straight. They also had the game's most dominant relief pitcher in Rich "Goose" Gossage.

The Goose was a fireballing workhorse. Unlike today's closers, who generally work only one inning, Gossage would often come in as early as the sixth or seventh inning and blow the opposition away. He had a league-leading twenty-seven saves for the 1978 Yanks, then pitched six scoreless innings in three World Series appearances. The Goose was going through a streak of wildness in the early days of 1979, but it was expected to be temporary.

Then came a game at Yankee Stadium against the Orioles on April 20. The Yanks lost, so tempers were a bit short when the team returned to the locker room to shower and dress. Gossage and second-string catcher Cliff Johnson were dressing across from one another when Gossage threw a small ball of rolled-up tape at Johnson—a typical clubhouse prank. The tape missed him, and big Cliff made a joke about Gossage's early-season wildness. Then Reggie Jackson asked the pitcher how Johnson had hit him when they were in the National League. Basically, Gossage said he couldn't. At that point, Johnson gave Gossage a playful—or not-so-playful—slap on the back of the head. From there, it was a case of boys will be boys.

Gossage thought the slap was too hard to be playful and threw a punch. Within seconds, the two big men were in an all-out, vicious brawl. It took several players and coaches to pull them apart. When the damages were assessed, it was the Yankee team that suffered the most.

It seems that Gossage had torn a ligament in the thumb of his pitching hand, a serious injury that required immediate surgery. He didn't return to the game until July 9. With no one to replace him in the bullpen, the Yanks faltered and were nearly out of the pennant race when Gossage returned. The team never quite regained its championship form and finished fourth.

The fight that shouldn't have happened cost both players the equivalent of ten days' pay in fines. It might even have cost the Yankees a chance at a third straight world championship.

We Won, Didn't We?

By all rights, the New York Yankees should have won the 1960 World Series in a walk over the Pittsburgh Pirates. Not only were the Yankees heavy favorites to capture yet another Fall Classic, but they proceeded to put on a record-breaking performance that is talked about to this day. There was one problem: they lost the series in seven games. Many people are still trying to figure out how it happened.

The Bronx Bombers of those years were really bombers. The team featured powerhouse hitters Mickey Mantle, Roger Maris, Yogi Berra, Moose Skowron, and Elston Howard, among others. They usually battered opponents into submission. But the Series against a good, scrappy Pittsburgh team took a strange twist. Games one, four, and five were all close, and the Pirates won each of them by scores of 6–4, 3–2, and 5–2. Games two, three, and six were one-sided, Bronx Bomber games. The Yanks won 16–3, 10–0, and 12–0. Total domination. Finally it came down to game seven to decide the champion.

Pittsburgh took an early 4–0 lead in the finale. Then the Bombers bounced back, their bats making it a 7–4 game by the eighth inning. It looked over, but the Pirates surprised everyone by scoring five runs in the bottom of the eighth to go ahead, 9–7. Once again, the Yanks came back, getting a pair in the top of the ninth to tie the game. If the Pirates couldn't score in their half of the ninth, the Series would run to extra innings.

But the decisive moment wasn't long in coming. Leading off the bottom of the ninth, Bucs second baseman Bill Mazeroski slammed Ralph Terry's second pitch into the left-field stands for a Series-winning home run. It was a dramatic finish to one of the strangest World Series ever.

Over the course of seven games, the Yankees outscored the Pirates, 55–27. They also outhit them, 91–60. That wasn't all. The Bombers set World Series records for total bases (142), the highest team batting average (.338), the most runs , most hits, and most runs batted-in (54). Yet they still lost! Someone looking over the stat sheets might logically ask, "Who goofed?" Couldn't the Yanks win close ones? Or was the deciding blooper Ralph Terry's gopher ball serve to Mazeroski? Maybe a little of both.

A Strange Place for a Nap

Talk about a "relaxed player." Cincinnati's Edd Roush gave that phrase new meaning during a game on June 8, 1920. A center fielder and fine hitter,

Roush was a star in baseball's early years and played each game to the hilt. He was a two-time National League batting champion who hit .300 or better for eleven straight seasons. His teammates called him a stubborn, hard-working player. But on this one day, Edd Roush must have simply forgotten where he was.

Roush was playing center field as the Reds battled the New York Giants at the Polo Grounds. In the eighth inning, the Giants' George Burns hit a bouncer over third base that umpire Barry McCormack called fair. The Cincinnati players went berserk. Catcher Ivy Wingo threw his glove in the air and was ejected from the game immediately. With that, all the other Cincy infielders charged at McCormack and began arguing about whether the ball was fair or foul.

In center field, Roush gave a sleepy yawn. He wasn't about to join the argument, so he put his glove and cap on the grass, used them as a pillow, and stretched out in the warm afternoon sun. The argument raged for several more minutes before order was finally restored and the field cleared. When umpire McCormack shouted, "Play Ball!" everyone was set . . . except Edd Roush. He was still flat out on the grass in center field. His teammates began shouting, but he didn't budge. During the argument, Roush had fallen into a deep sleep.

Finally, third baseman Heinie Groh walked over and woke up the sleeping star. As Roush got drowsily to his feet, the first thing he saw was McCormack thumbing him out of the game. That *really* woke him up, and another argument raged. The umpire's decision held, and Edd Roush was thrown out of the game for falling asleep. Reds' manager Pat Moran never understood the ejection.

"A lot of players have been caught sleeping on plays, and they don't get the boot."

Rock-a-Bye Freddie

It was spring training in 1927, and Freddie Fitzsimmons was getting ready for another season. Known as "Fat" Freddie because of his constant battles with the bulge, Fitzsimmons was a fine right-handed pitcher who won 217 games in a nineteen-year career. He was getting ready for his third season and working hard in the Miami heat. One evening, after a hard day's workout and big dinner, a sleepy Fitzsimmons sat down in a rocking chair on the front porch of the hotel where the team was staying.

A couple of teammates joined him and began chatting. Within a few minutes, Fitzsimmons had fallen asleep. He was even beginning to snore while his teammates chuckled. They watched him for a few minutes, then got a shock when Fat Freddie suddenly let out a loud scream and clutched his pitching hand. What in the world could have happened?

It seems that as he dozed and rocked, his right arm fell off his lap and dangled at the side of the chair. Somehow, his fingers found their way under the rung of the rocker, which passed right over them. The fingers weren't broken, but they were bruised enough for Freddie to miss a number of his April starts. One of baseball's strangest injuries could have cost the Giants the pennant that year. When the season ended, the New Yorkers were two games behind the Pirates. Fitzsimmons won seventeen, but had he not missed those April starts, who knows?

"When he rocked on his hand, we laughed at him," said teammate Bill Terry, who witnessed the strange accident. "But there weren't many of us laughing about it when the season was over."

Chapter 6

So This Is Baseball

Over the years there have been so many crazy, offbeat happenings in baseball that it's impossible to write about all of them. It turns out that any baseball game—whether the seventh game of the World Series or a late-August game between two losing teams—can suddenly produce a legendary moment. Here is a potpourri of wild and wacky bloopers that have occurred through the years. Enjoy them—and remember, they really happened.

A Long Vigil

Some baseball fans center their entire lives on their favorite team. Unlike a player, who can affect the outcome of a game or pennant race with his arm or his bat, fans can only cheer and hope their team comes out on top. A few, however, have tried to help their teams in bizarre ways. Take the case of Charley Lupica.

He was a rabid Cleveland Indians fan who was in his glory when the Tribe won the 1948 American League pennant and World Series. Unfortunately, the next year, instead of looking as if they would repeat their success, the Indians got off to a horrible start and were floundering in seventh place. Lupica decided to take some radical action.

On May 31, Lupica announced he was going to climb a flagpole in Cleveland and perch there until the Indians were once again in first place. It was a bad move. Although the Indians did improve, it was soon apparent they would not repeat their winning streak. Nonetheless, Lupica stayed the course. Finally, after 117 days atop the flagpole, he was persuaded to come down. By the way, the Indians finished third.

An Even Longer Vigil

In the early 1900s, the Chicago Cubs had one of the best teams in the National League. They had the legendary double-play combination of Joe Tinker, Johnny Evers, and Frank Chance; a star outfielder in "Wildfire" Schulte; and star pitchers "Three Finger" Brown and Ed Ruelbach. This team nucleus helped the Cubs to National League pennants in 1906, 1907, 1908, and 1910. In 1907 and 1908 the Cubbies won the World Series.

Today the Cubs remain in Chicago as one of the league's oldest and most stable franchises. There's only one problem. The Cubs haven't won a World Series since 1908! It's the longest championship drought in major-league history. The team has challenged several times, but they've fallen short. They did reach the World Series in 1918, 1929, 1932, 1935, 1938, and 1945, but they always blew the chance to return a championship banner to Wrigley Field.

Now it has been more than half a century since the Cubbies have even reached the Series. Yet their faithful fans keep coming out year after year, wondering what kinds of bloopers will keep their beloved Cubs from winning again.

One of the Best Games Ever Lost

On September 15, 1969, the St. Louis Cardinals went up against the New York Mets. For the Mets, an expansion team in 1962, it was a magical year. They would rise from seasons of finishing last to win the pennant and then the World Series. But on this particular night, they faced a future Hall of Fame pitcher at the top of his game.

Lefty Steve Carlton was in his fifth season, a year in which he would win seventeen games and strike out 210 hitters. On this night, everything was working for him. He fanned one Met after another and appeared to have a shot at the then all-time record of eighteen strikeouts in a nine-inning game. When the game ended, Carlton had indeed set a new record by striking out nineteen Mets hitters. There was only one problem. He lost the game!

Among Carlton's strikeout victims that night was

Steven Carlton is a Hall of Famer who won 329 games during his career. Pitching for the Cardinals in 1969, Carlton set a then major-league record by striking out nineteen Mets. Unfortunately, he lost the game on a pair of two-run homers by Ron Swoboda.

Mets' right fielder Ron Swoboda. Carlton whiffed him twice. In Swoboda's two other at bats, however, Carlton committed perhaps his only bad pitches of the game. Each of those times, Swoboda came to bat with a runner on base, and each time he whacked a two-run homer to clinch the win for the Mets.

Carlton would retire with 329 victories, four Cy Young Awards, and more than four thousand career strikeouts, second on the all-time list. But on one September night, when he had all the right stuff, two bad pitches did him in—and he fell victim to the magic that was the miracle Mets.

What a Way to Start a Season

Big Don Drysdale was one of the best pitchers of the 1950s and 1960s, a mean sidearmer who would prefer to hit a batter rather than let the batter hit one of his pitches. He would win 209 games in his fourteen-year career before arm problems led to his retirement at age thirty-three.

Like all pitchers, Drysdale seemed to be off to a good start when he was chosen to be the Dodgers' opening-day pitcher on April 7, 1969. The Dodgers were playing Cincinnati. First up was Pete Rose, a great hitter but not a real slugger. Drysdale wound up and fired the first pitch of the year. Rose jumped on it and sent it sailing over the left-field wall for a home run.

Drysdale couldn't believe it. One pitch, one homer. Next up was Bobby Tolan, and Drysdale probably thought long and hard about throwing the first pitch to Tolan. In those days, a batter who came up after a teammate's home run was often chased away from home plate by a hard inside pitch. But Drysdale figured he had better establish the strike zone. So he started Tolan with another fastball.

Whack! Tolan jumped on the pitch and sent it deep into the right-field bleachers. Two pitches, two home runs—both by players who hadn't hit a single round-tripper during the entire spring training. This had never happened before.

Being the competitor that he was, Drysdale settled down and didn't allow another run, and the Dodgers won, 3–2. Still, he couldn't believe that he opened the season with two very fat pitches.

"Let's just say [the home runs] woke me up real quick," Drysdale later said.

Can a Blooper Be Good?

Norm Cash was a good first baseman on some very good Detroit Tigers teams in the 1960s. But not even Stormin' Norman could have predicted the kind of season he would put together in 1961. Cash looked like the second coming of Lou Gehrig all year long. When the season ended he had won the American League batting title with an impressive .361 mark. Add to that 41 home runs and 132 RBIs, and you have a season to remember.

Cash was just twenty-six years old and in his fourth season, so there was no reason to believe he wasn't a superstar in the making. As it turned out, the '61 season was his career blooper. The following year, facing most of the same pitchers and using the same bat, Cash only hit .243—a drop of 118 points from his batting average. He still managed 39 homers, but his RBIs dropped to 89.

In fact, in seventeen big-league seasons, Norm Cash never hit .300 again. He never drove home 100 runs, and he rarely approached the 193 hits he had in that one incredible season. Cash retired a solid player with a .271 lifetime average and 377 homers. But his one super year was a blooper.

There Are Injuries, and Then There Are Injuries

It's a rare big-leaguer who doesn't get hurt at some time in his career. A pulled hamstring, twisted ankle, torn rotator cuff, rib cage injury—these are just some of the hazards of the game. Then there are the freak injuries, the ones that don't occur in the line of duty. One such blooper might have cost the St. Louis Cardinals a world championship in 1985.

Outfielder Vince Coleman was a speedy twenty-four-year-old rookie that year. During the regular season, Coleman stole an amazing 110 bases. Then came the playoffs. The Cards had to face the L.A. Dodgers in the National League championship series.

Before the fourth game, which was played at Busch Stadium in St. Louis, the Cards were working out. At the end of the workout, the grounds crew began rolling the tarp out to cover the field. Vince Coleman was still on the field and had his back turned to the crew. Suddenly, something hit him, knocking him down. The huge, heavy roller that held the tarp had passed over his left leg. The resulting injury finished his season.

Though the Cards went on to defeat the Dodgers, they blew a 3–1 lead in the Series and lost to the Kansas City Royals in seven games. Had the speedy Coleman been in there, the results may well have been different. The rookie swiped 110 bases but couldn't get out of the way of a slow-moving tarpaulin roller.

Where's Home Plate?

People sometimes tend to forget that talented athletes possess a rare gift—an ability to play a sport on a much higher level than the rest of us. Athletes should also realize how quickly that gift can disappear. Most times, when an athlete suddenly "loses it," it's the result of an injury. A torn rotator cuff, severe ligament damage to a knee, a career-ending neck injury. It's what every top athlete fears.

Sometimes the gift disappears for no apparent reason. Steve Blass is a perfect example. He was a talented right-handed pitcher for the Pittsburgh Pirates for ten years—at least, that's how long his career lasted; the talented part was only the first eight years. After that, Blass became one of baseball's great unsolved mysteries.

Up to that point, Blass seemed to be getting better and better. In his fourth season, 1968, he was 18–6. He won 16 the next year and then was 15–8 with a 2.85 earned-run average in the Pirates' pennant-winning year of 1971. He was brilliant in the World Series against Baltimore, going 2–0 with a 1.00 ERA, giving up just seven hits in eighteen innings and winning the seventh and final game.

A year later, 1972, the thirty-year-old Blass seemed on the verge of superstardom, going 19–8 with a 2.49 ERA. He had fine control, walking just 84 batters in nearly 250 innings of work. When he returned for the 1973 season, however, he was suddenly a different pitcher.

For some reason, Blass just couldn't or wouldn't unleash his fine fastball. Even worse, his control was completely gone. Not only couldn't he find the plate, he was actually throwing behind some hitters. The walks piled up while his victories were almost nonexistent, and his earned-run average ballooned to almost ten runs per game.

Blass said there was no pain or stiffness in his arm. Yet he seemed almost fearful of pitching. He finished the year with a dismal 3–9 record and a 9.85 ERA. Unbelievably, a pitcher who a year earlier had walked just 84 hitters in 250 innings now walked 84 in just 88.2 innings. Blass tried everything to regain his winning form, including psychotherapy and even transcendental meditation.

He pitched only one game in 1974, walking seven and giving up five hits in just five innings. He was then sent to the minors, where things just got worse. Steve Blass retired from baseball at age thirty-two. His sudden loss of form was a blooper, a mystery no one could solve.

Bad-Luck Bobo

Bobo Newsom was one of the most notable pitchers in baseball history. He was a workhorse who pitched in the majors for twenty years, throwing his last game when he was forty-six years old. Bobo played for nine teams and wore seventeen uniforms. He was with the Washington Senators on five different occasions. And his lifetime win/loss mark of 211–222 makes him one of only two pitchers to win more than 200 games but lose even more.

One of Bobo's problems was bad luck. He was a walking blooper, an accident looking for a place to happen. Injuries weren't only part of his game—sometimes they seemed to *be* his game. During his career he had more than his share of broken bones. Many times, however, his injuries also showcased his toughness.

Take opening day of 1936. Bobo and the Senators were up against the New York Yankees. President Franklin Roosevelt threw out the first ball, and many Washington dignitaries sat in the stands. Bobo wanted to pitch well. In the third inning, one of the Yanks hit a slow roller to third. The Senators' Ossie Bluege charged the ball, picked it up barehanded, and fired hard toward first. On the mound, Bobo forgot a cardinal rule on a play like that. The pitcher is supposed to duck to give the third baseman a clear throw to first. Instead, the ball slammed into the side of Bobo's face, breaking his jaw and knocking him out. Incredibly, he stayed in the game and went on to beat Lefty Gomez and the Yanks, 1–0.

Said Newsom later, "When the president of the United States comes out to see ol' Bobo pitch, ol' Bobo ain't gonna let him down."

Another time, Bobo had his kneecap shattered by

Bobo Newsom won 211 games pitching for nine teams and trading uniforms seventeen times in twenty years. He also had all kinds of bad luck, like suffering a broken jaw and being knocked out when he forgot to duck as his third baseman winged a throw to first. Characteristically, Bobo chose to play out the game. He won it, 1–0.

a line drive, yet he finished pitching the game before having his leg put in a cast for several weeks. On yet another occasion, he fell asleep at the wheel while driving and plunged his car over a 225-foot (68.5 m) embankment. The result, another broken leg.

Shortly after he had the cast off, he attended a mule auction near his home in Hartsville, South Carolina. One of the mules wound up and kicked Bobo in his bad leg, breaking it once again. Then there was the time in 1940 when he tripped in the dugout, landing on the concrete floor and suffering a back injury that kept him out of action for several weeks.

Bad-luck Bobo could also be a danger to his teammates. Returning to the Senators in 1947, Bobo had a teammate named George Case, who was trying to get an injured shoulder back in shape. He was just about ready to go when Bobo came happily into the dugout and gave Case a playful, but hard, slap on the back. Guess what? Yep. The slap injured Case's shoulder all over again.

That was Bobo Newsom, a walking blooper.

Fogged Out

One of the strangest postponements in baseball history occurred on May 20, 1960, when the Chicago Cubs were playing the Milwaukee Braves at County Stadium in Milwaukee. Early in the game the fog began rolling in, and it kept getting worse, a weather blooper if there ever was one. By the fifth inning it had become so bad that there was talk of stopping the game.

Finally, with the Braves batting in the last of the fifth, umpire Frank Dascoli decided to test the fog. All four umpires went to the outfield, where the three Cubs fielders were waiting. Then Frank Thomas of the Cubs was asked to hit a fungo (a fly ball) to the outfield. Thomas complied. When none of the umpires and none of the three outfielders could see the ball, Dascoli decided to call the game. It was officially fogged out, a scoreless tie.

Gnats Can Do the Trick, Too

Fog may seem like a strange reason to postpone a game, but an even stranger one occurred at Ebbets Field in Brooklyn during the second game of a doubleheader between the Cubs and the Dodgers on September 15, 1946. Sometime after the game was under way, swarms of gnats began descending on the ballpark. They were bothering the players and fans alike. Soon, it was getting hard for anyone to concentrate on baseball. Everyone was busy trying to shoo the flying insects away.

By the sixth inning, despite the perfect sunshiny September weather, it was becoming impossible to play baseball. Although the gnats were a serious problem, the fans themselves brought the game to a standstill. They were so bothered by the insects that many began waving their white scorecards around to ward off the gnats. All that white in the outfield hampered the batters' vision.

Finally, the umpires had had enough. The game was called after six innings, with the Dodgers winning, 2–0. It was treated the same as a rain-out. Only this time it was a gnat-out.

A Present Mom Didn't Want

Talk about being in the wrong place at the right time. On Mother's Day in 1939, Cleveland Indians ace Bob Feller asked his parents to come to Chicago to watch him pitch against the White Sox. He figured a victory would be a nice present for Mom, then all three could have dinner together. Rapid Robert got his parents good seats on the first-base line and went to work.

In the third inning he was facing Chicago third sacker Marv Owen. Feller threw his fabled fastball, and Owen couldn't get around on it. He hit a line drive foul behind first base. Believe it or not, the ball made a beeline for Mrs. Feller's head. It broke her glasses and caused a cut that would require six stitches to close.

A distraught Feller raced over to see if his mother was all right. When she insisted she was okay and that he return to the mound, Feller then struck Owen out and completed a 9–4 victory. But it wasn't quite the present for his mom that he had in mind.

A Big Wind Indoors

The Kansas City Royals were playing the Seattle Mariners in the Seattle Kingdome on May 27, 1981, when KC's Amos Otis topped a slow roller toward third. The ball was rolling much too slowly for third baseman Lenny Randle to make a play. He could only hope it would roll foul.

Suddenly, Randle had an idea. He dropped down onto his hands and knees, leaned forward, and literally blew the ball foul. At first, umpire Larry McCoy fell for the ruse and called Otis back. But when Royals manager Jim Frey protested, the umps cited a rule that says a player cannot alter the course of a ball and called it a hit.

"I didn't blow on it," Randle later said. "I just used the power of suggestion. I was telling the ball to roll foul."

But Seattle's public relations director, Bob Porter, laughed at Randle's explanation. "We don't have any wind in our indoor stadium," he said. "But that night we had a breeze, and it was created by Lenny Randle."

This One Was Really a Lemon

In the early days of baseball there were no lights at the ballpark. Once daylight began to fade, it was time to call the game. One afternoon, before the turn of the century, Baltimore was playing Washington in a National League game. The game ran late, and darkness was approaching quickly. Orioles catcher Wilbert Robinson wanted the game called, but umpire Jack Kerns insisted it continue.

Finally, Robinson decided to pull a fast one. He walked out to the mound to talk to his pitcher, John Clarkson. While talking, he took a lemon from his pocket and gave it to the pitcher. "Throw this on the next pitch," he insisted. Clarkson smiled and nodded.

Sure enough, Clarkson slipped the baseball into his back pocket and fired the lemon toward home plate. It smacked into Robinson's mitt, and umpire Kerns roared, "Strike one!" without hesitation. Robinson then called time, whirled around to Kerns, and opened his glove. There was the lemon.

"When you can't tell the difference between a

baseball and a lemon, it's time to stop playing," Robby said. Kerns turned a few shades of red, a combination of anger and embarrassment, but he had to agree. The game was called because of darkness.

A Fishy Rain-Out

Players have tried many tricks to get an umpire to stop a game. Back in 1908, a steady rain began falling during a contest between Cleveland and Detroit. Hall of Fame umpire Tommy Connolly was behind the plate when Tiger infielder Germany Schaefer began to complain about the rain. He wanted the game stopped, but Connolly refused.

When Detroit took the field for the next inning, Schaefer came out of the dugout wearing high rubber boots, a raincoat, and a wide-brimmed rain hat, then opened an umbrella. When Connolly demanded to know what was going on, Schaefer replied, "I have a very bad cold, and it's now bordering on pneumonia. If I get rid of my rubber boots, raincoat, and umbrella, I will be in the hospital in less than two hours, and I will certainly sue you and the league."

Connolly looked around at the rain, the field, and Schaefer. Then he laughed and suspended play.

The Babe's Blooper Equals Perfection

It seems only fitting to conclude this book with yet another story about Babe Ruth. Although he is the most legendary of all baseball players, the Babe wasn't perfect. Occasionally he let his temper get the best of him. One time, the Babe's temper led to one of the greatest pitching performances ever.

It happened on June 23, 1917, when the young Babe was still a star pitcher for the Boston Red Sox. Ruth started against Washington that day and promptly walked the first batter who faced him. When umpire Brick Owens called ball four, the Babe thought the pitch was a strike and became enraged. He charged home plate, stuck his face into the umpire's, and began arguing like a madman. Owens tried to calm him down but couldn't. The ump had no choice but to thumb the Babe out of the game.

Right-hander Ernie Shore was then summoned from the bullpen. After warming up, Shore got set to pitch. As he faced his first hitter, the runner on first took off and was promptly thrown out stealing. Shore then retired the batter plus the next one to end the inning.

In fact, Shore retired all twenty-six batters he faced. Because the first runner was thrown out stealing, Shore was given credit for a perfect game— a pitching gem that is quite a rarity. In fact, it's the only perfect game in baseball history that wasn't a complete game.

Shore had to thank the one and only Babe Ruth for his great pitching performance. Without the Babe losing his temper and committing a childish blooper, Shore might never have gotten into the game and made baseball history.